The Evolutionary Purpose of Heartbreak

For Lauren —
Hope you find
some pleasure in these
pages!
Joanne

The Evolutionary Purpose of Heartbreak

Poems by ~~Joanne~~ Harris Allred

Joanne allred

Turning Point

Published by Turning Point Press
P.O. Box 541106
Cincinnati, OH 45254-1106

ISBN: 9781625490216
LCCN: 2013937513

Poetry Editor: Kevin Walzer
Business Editor: Lori Jareo

Visit us on the web at www.turningpointbooks.com

Author photo by Ray Harris
Cover design by Beth Spencer

Cover image:
Georgia O'Keeffe Red and Pink, 1925 Oil on
canvas; 40.6 x 31.8 cm (16 x 12 1/2 in.) framed:
61.2 x 52.5 x 4 cm (24 1/8 x 20 11/16 x 1 9/16 in.)
Harvard Art Museums/Fogg Museum, Gift of Dr.
Ernest G. Stillman, Class of 1907, by exchange,
2006.49 Photo: Imaging Department © President and
Fellows of Harvard College

Acknowledgments

Thanks to the editors of magazines in which these
poems first appeared:

City Arts, "What You Think Love Is" (as "Boundaries")
Eclipse, "Bleat," "Early Light"
Pearl, "The Fool"
Santa Clara Review, "Pleasantown"
South Dakota Review, "Sun Enters Pisces"
Women's Review of Books, "Shameless"

"A Bird in the Hand," was published as part of a hand-printed
poetry card project by Quoin Collective.

"General Store, Garrison Utah," was part of a collaborative
poetry-art installation, with artist Carla Resnick, at 1078 Gallery.
"Two Lines Borrowed" and "Early Narcissus" appeared in
Chico News and Review as part of their Poetry 99 Project.

"Pleasantown" was reprinted in *From Dusk to Need, 25 Years of
Flume Press*, 2010.

Much gratitude to early readers of this collection for invaluable
suggestions: thank you for your wisdom and generous
friendship Jeanne Clark, Carole Oles, Beth Spencer, Gary
Thompson, and Deborah Woodard. Thanks also to the many
who encourage me in my work and nourish my life including,
but not limited to, Danielle Alexich, Carolyn Ayres, Marian
Baldy, Scott Cairns, Jackie Chavis, Janese Charpentier, Liz
Harris, Heart of the Lotus Sangha, George Keithley, Barbara
Kniffin, Jessica MacKenzie, Josh McKinney, Kathleen
McPartland, Sharon Paquin, Marilyn Ringer, John Travis, Rose
Tripp, Susan Wooldridge. Jerry, your love and support mean
everything. Julie, Gary, AnneMarie, Jake, Vicky, Briana, Nell,
you are precious to me beyond words.

For my mother, Virginia Harris,
and in memory of my father,
Glenn Harris

Table of Contents

III
Living in Flesh

The way is not in the sky.   The way is in the heart.

Buddha, as quoted in *The Dhammapada*

I

Each Beauty Stung with a Promise

Bitten

When did you last eat an apple
under moonlight, the bitten globe
in the sky a twin to that in your hand?
The crickets and tree toads rocking
the night lull you into believing
you've found your one true home.
A bullfrog down in the draw
where a stream is drying to summer
fallow sounds its bassoon. The woodwind
of a great-horned owl hushes the hillside.
Bristling in the scrub behind you
may be a doe with fawn
or something serpentine.
Yes, you've heard it all before.
The present is an old, old story.
But for the few moments you munch
the apple, the world seems so fresh
it all remains to be written.

Early Light

Swaths of mist gauze the hillside where
two white-rumped forms the size of jackrabbits
bound in the tall, drying grass.
Laid back ears.

From behind the brush a doe appears.
She dips her head to nuzzle
the smaller fawn then allows
them both to suckle.

There's a story of a dying monk, at last
complete and poised to merge with the infinite,

who, with his final breath,
remembers a stag
in a field at sunrise
and instantly incarnates as a deer.

The doe is on the move now, fawns
tottering after, prancing every few steps
to keep up, exuberant. They browse
into the woods and vanish.

Was it the soul's yearning after beauty
that drew the dying man back into a body?

Or did his heart crack
open, as mine just did,
wanting somehow to keep
this fleet tenderness.

Rapture

I hang sheets to dry in the light breeze,
the lavender scent of laundry soap mingling
with honeysuckle vining a post,
the day the world is scheduled to end.
Redwing blackbirds flit and chitter
in new-minted oaks, bringing to the nest
mayfly, caterpillar. I watch a pair
of honeybees in friendly consort
ruffling the corolla of a deep purple
thistle. It's an ordinary day
marked only by the rapture of the mundane,
which makes yearning for a more exalted realm
seem both ungrateful and blind.
A lone mallard, his mate off nesting
in undisclosed reeds, paddles the pond
quibbling, head emerald, white and ultra-
marine on his tucked wings. When he flies,
riffles unsettle the perfect surface,
lapping shore long after he vanishes
over cottonwoods quaking along the creek.

How the Story Ends

Maybe he woke up thinking, as we often did in 1984,
about Ronald Reagan's finger poised above the button,
hearing the thunder roll of a thousand nuts
and bolts poured slowly from a pail
to simulate a fraction of the nukes
waiting for launch. I remember
wanting to unknow what I knew, to go back
to sleep, not having to work anymore
for a world beyond war.
The night I heard myself say
we each have to decide if we are for life or death
and I choose life my daughter was conceived.
That was the year I read *Out on a Limb*
and tried on being an immortal soul, my body
ripe with the same emptiness
that plumps out the universe.
On hands and knees on the kitchen floor
searching for a dropped needle after
my brother-in-law shot himself that January,
it came to me that perhaps we all, in some way, choose
our deaths: driving off Lookout Point
rather than, say, eating one more marbled steak
or smoking another pack, the choice
is more transparent and the bluntness shocks.
So reading the news that after nineteen
years in a coma a man woke up,
I wonder if all this time he has been out deliberating,
a jury of one: live or die, go or stay, knowing
the brain's imperatives must be wholly reconfigured.
Even if he weren't quadriplegic now
he couldn't cradle his baby daughter again.

But neither can I hold mine.
And sometimes looking at her—nineteen!—
it seems so discontinuous: my arms
still tingle with her smallness.
The past is brindled with amnesia,
each memory a rogue particle of fevered
omniscience that knows how the story ends.

Each Beauty Stung by a Promise

At the creek a Golden Eye with a dozen ducklings
the size of tennis balls paddles about in the shallows.

She chatters steadily to keep them trailing. Two
or three clamber onto her back for a ride.

One is left behind on the bank among the rocks
and broom. Peeping so softly its mother doesn't notice.

When my children were small we raised a pair
of mallards in the pond behind the house.

Wilbur, the hen, had been missing for days—
we'd feared her lost to fox, coyote or raccoon—

until the morning she waddled quacking from the reeds
with ten dandelion puffs following.

Each day for a week we watched the flock
diminish until there were just two ducklings.

Days later, none. Finally even Wilbur's russet
feathers we found strewn beside the water.

Now this mother duck, with her tenuous
entourage, swims for the other shore.

Hawk Flight

Over Flat-iron Ridge two red-tails
tunnel the dusk, their cries bruising
the bluff rock. Climbing late summer
thermals their wings rise and thin,
struck matches going out
suddenly in evening's slate pool.

Seeing them slip into depths
not visible feels like a kind of drowning—
some element I can't breathe closes
overhead and leaves me knowing
not the hawks' destination, but my own
limitation: how slim a margin
of light human vision admits.

My friend went out abruptly like that—
you might say from out of the blue.
Death broke unexpectedly onto the scene,
a black-clad figure riding into focus,
closing quickly over a plain.
Where the horse stepped across,
the border shivered like a mirage.

One day we spoke of such mysteries,
holed up in our windowless office
like hushed agents underground
careful of betraying our cover.
She told me how, when her mother lay
dying, a lone rider had appeared
on the range where a cow was calving.

She spurred to meet the trespasser, a woman
she determined, before a chill
of recognition reined her. The familiar
tilt of the hat and cut of the coat—
the way it angled off her shoulders—
and the resemblance of the mare to one
her mother favored, said *stay away, let it be.*

As my friend lay in ICU, with tubes
and machines doing the work of choked
organs, I thought of her riding
at her ranch near Greenville. Timothy rises
fresh past the withers. Thunderheads
mass over Mount Lassen as she canters
towards the rain.

Winter Landscape

In late winter sun, the old silo throws an indigo slash
across untracked snow. Where, in this weather,

could a tractor go anyway? Purposes break down
like the jagged fence slats snapped by wind or

the weight of snowdrift or by creatures blind in a blizzard
wanting out or in. A piece missing from everything

like the moon just clearing the horizon.
Who hasn't wandered such a field?—markers buried,

the known lost to a memory
of wildflowers blazing, a child running across grass.

Struck by a car she is gone even before the ambulance
arrives. A twenty-year marriage cracks in the cold.

What sign posts then? Your own fist raised in a howl
is the only lantern you can follow. A blood-red

barn scarcely warms the darkening landscape.

Early Narcissus

At the small gathering in a country cemetery
where his daughter's ashes are finally interred,
he says every day he fingers the husk

of her absence. Three years
since she took her young life: the door to her
room shut, artifacts still undisturbed.

It's winter and cold, as it should be.
After the others leave, he sits on frosted
grass until well after dusk, content

to let an owl be the voice of fog
swathing skeletal trees. Shrouds of moonlight
brighten the mist. Near the gate, leathery fins

of early narcissus are already breaching ground—
relentless life crushing up from oblivion.

Sun Enters Pisces

Small hands of the morning rain
drum anxiously that old
doubt of blue, not exactly song
or warning, upon the shingles.
An explosion of white down along
a gravel shoulder marks where a truck
ended a swan's northern migration,
an atrocity of our day-to-day
civility, which doesn't stir
underground spores, dormant,
not dead. The weight of winter unpeels
flesh from bone in little tortures.
The breathless green sentence
is punctuated now by an occasional
bright daffodil, its fever-dream
yellow anticipating God the way
the good soul who planted bulbs
along the roadside when all was dying
believed in this disinterested resurrection.

Two Lines Borrowed

You were once a swan singing
north, one voice in a chorus, holding
your place like a high note
in a wavering formation.
You gave yourself up
to the movement
of seasons, the lengthening days,
to the magnetic force pulling you elsewhere.
Of course there was a destination,
but it was no concern.
You were simply wingstroke and song.
There was the surge of spring—everything
suddenly growing again—and it was inside you
too, lifting. The flock was of one mind
that dawn it wheeled from the lake
where you'd wintered: one
with the pale sky, the pearly haze
where only birdcall is distinct in the hush
before the rising sun.

Pleasantown

Morning breeze off the sleepy orchard
unravels mares' tails whispering
of ocean: cloud speech, feathery fricatives
never really separate from any other syllable
of motion. Beneath the ground surface
tree roots crisscross, converse
as do ripening apples calling red to the blue
jays. We break the spectrum

here, saying *Jonathan, Delicious,*
there, *apricot, peach,*
distinctions of the human palate
which paints the world to suit a taste
for separation. Neither
the plant kingdom nor the wind knows
loneliness, although we hear it
in the weeping birch, in clouds shuffling
over the day like indecision.

I have set you apart, married you
to someone else, called you indifferent
just to name this urge for what's
inaccessible. So I invent my longing
to connect, perhaps not with you after all
but with some absence you suggest.
In a dream you move to a place called
Pleasantown, leave without saying goodbye.

Lost Seasons

i.
This morning cobwebs tremble on the pane,
strings of an instrument you once knew
how to play. A hushed lament fades
into the monotone green of a weeping
willow, throaty but pure. Nothing's empty of potential,
every stirring translucence invites you to hum along.
These cheeping birds are years that slipped away,
the breeze a dwelling you've wished for
but could never afford. That cottage overlooking
the Pacific is just one of infinite possibilities.
But you must choose soon, before the fog closes
its fist and those dreamy sheep grazing
the hillside become small boats lost at sea,
bleating. The headlands are not open for discussion,
each hastening toward its appointed anguish.

ii.
You hear a background swishing, like a toilet running
in another part of the house or someone outside
watering the wilted lobelia, a sound absent-minded
like trees, impossible to render precisely.
You mean to come back to the meaning of things,
but the long daylight liquefies, ice tinkling in a glass.
Foreshortened darkness must make do for now,
adumbrations all but ignored in patterns of the ample
leaves and in plump pockets of the fragrant woods,
just as small but maturing shadows inhabit you
and all the others seeking respite in afternoon shade.
The winnowing period saunters nearer, a phase
of sparseness and introspection, when letting go

will tax all your generosity, and stars
will tap their beaks, hungry, at the window.

iii.
Time stopped the month before everything died,
as if a vote had been taken by weary farmers,
impatient with silage, saying *enough*. Black birds
still formed their regiments along the phone wires,
which had relinquished their high-pitched whining.
Some conclusion had been collectively drawn
and duly recorded, a metaphor so obscure
not even the itinerant gum-shoe or Sibylian
schoolmarm could fathom its referent.
There persisted common routines like eating supper
and shitting upon waking, but, along with desire,
color had leached from the landscape.
Like an old man with a few threads of gray hair
who has no ambition to better himself,
nor offers so much as a wave in passing.

iv.
Life on the road is the gist of wind's melody,
a fleeting reminiscence of wild roses
that bloomed in stifling sweetness and,
in the end, stank along no one's cedar fence,
hips sinking into a frost-etched rubble
of spotted leaves, like a sigh after a good meal,
a mild acceptance. Then some urgent gust
turned us around and with faces stiff we hurried
off to discover a new terrain
of denial, suspense like a brakeless truck singing
down a mountainside. In the smelter
of human busyness burns a craving
for the infinite. Sooner or later a calm rusticity

returns like honeysuckle suffusing the night,
whose love gestures toward dark distance and long sleep.

A Bird in the Hand

A galaxy's etched upon his neck ruff,
delicate black-on-white ellipses.
Head canted right, as if questioning
his fate. *What was that* he must have wondered
between window and death. Ebony plume
curled sideways. When he hit, the glass rattled.
I saw him frantically clawing air,
gathered him up in time to feel the wild pulse
fail, hunted eyes softly closing. Heavier
in my hand than I'd have imagined.
Heavier in my heart. I saw him once, brave
sentry, perched on a bench near the pond
while a mother and her young crept out
to drink, then quail-scurried into the bush.

Bleat

One day in late May they are suddenly gone,
six spring lambs we've tracked, the dogs
and I, on our walks past their field.

I've made a habit of counting, a game
of spotting them hidden beneath the willows
where they liked to lie in a heap or
in the sheltering lee of their dams' shadows.

How quickly they fattened on milk
and sweet meadow grass, from spindly-
legged wobblers to gamboling wool balls,
nearing half the size of their mothers.

The three shorn ewes remain, heads
bent to earth where the graze
is already browning. One stands apart,

lifting to gaze around through dumb,
slotted eyes, her teats still sagging.
Her bleat is a knell—the sound
of absence, of grief, of unrelieved need,

the wild and delicate interior of an old hunger.

What Burns

I've been thinking October's sweetness
is like the violins in Tchaikovsky's *Pathetique,*
a rapture of sadness keening down
the neck of shortening time.
But the crimson burning this curtain
of grape leaves is no finale.
The window it covers is opening.

From a distance, subtler harmonies fruit
on the wind, as if hearing has grown
more acute, the volume turned up on desire.
Scraps of flame drift to earth, graceful
as the skeins of geese threading south.
Today even breath seems an answer to prayer,
a constant letting go the outworn, the over.

Smoke

Smoke and Mirrors

And on the third day, the duration a spirit shocked
from its breathless body is said to keep
vigil over its beloved jail, freed
but still attached to being attached,
the sky clears to sapphire, leaving
only charred hillsides and the enduring scent
of burned woods. The confused ghosts
of suddenly-taken trees and brush
depart, simply disappear.

Burning Bridges

The fire jumps Butte Creek below the Covered Bridge
then guns up the hillside crackling toward us.
It's the theoretical question played live:
You have minutes to evacuate, what will you take?

Not much. Fresh underwear, toothbrush,
prescription meds. Diplomas, passports,
zip drive, laptop, notebook and pen,
a duffle stuffed with photos. Two dogs, leashes,
and eight hens crammed in a wire crate. A little cash
kept in the house, a few gold coins.

I forget the small clay jar, painted
and fired by a Zuni potter, on a shelf
by the bathroom sink: a gift
from my husband after one grueling summer,
safekeeping my diamond ring.

Fighting Fire with Fire

On the hillside above our house, fighters light
a back blaze to halt advancing flames.
When wind swells, the back-fire backfires,
engulfing the bluff, leaping the highway,
taking out several unsuspecting homes.

Who hasn't made such a miscalculation?
A blow-up, they call it.
An incendiary remark, fiery words thrown back
in defense. Caught by an untamed gust, anyone's house
can be torched to the ground, destroyed.

Shoveling Smoke

Fire crews still work the canyon, but bombers
dropping crimson slurry and helicopters dangling
enormous water buckets no longer shudder over.
It feels less like a war zone today.
They are attending residual hotspots with shovels,
gathering up hoses strewn and abandoned in a flurry.
I unwind hot-pink panic tape
from mailbox and gate. Dusty
albums go back in the bookcase: burnt scent
of memory, gray duff of time dissolved.

Smoke Signals

Power has been restored, phone lines
restrung, though the cell-phone tower that went
down is still down. A rash of email asks
if our house is still standing, offering a place to stay.
Our closed road was featured on national news.
We are fine! So blessed, I reply,
a smoke screen for sadness
smoldering inside. Not survivor's guilt
exactly, not my faith gone up in smoke, but a singeing
brush with destiny. The pervasiveness of ash.

Blowing Smoke

Sir Walter Raleigh won a measure of gold
from the Queen by concocting a means
to weigh smoke: he figured the difference between
tobacco balanced on one scale side and, on the other, ash
from his pipe after smoking the equivalent.
Like measuring the weight of the soul, Harvey Keitel
says in the movie, *Smoke*. 21 grams
a human body is said to lighten at death.

No way to measure the mass of life that chokes
the air, darkens our lungs, weights our spirits.

Smoke Made with the Fumes of Sighs

A ten-year-old lights the cigarette filched
from his uncle's coat pocket, innocent urge
to taste the wild flaring out of control.
Bent mower blade strikes a rock.
Wind snaps a power pole.

Some sicko waits for just this day when gusts
ride a tiger's fury, prowling with gas can
and matches. Heat crouches in parched grass,
panting, ready to spring. In the language
of fire *love* is *summer field.*

Where There's Smoke

If the Big Bang Theory is correct,
we are all, and everything,
made wholly of smoke
from that primal conflagration:
residue of cosmic pyrolosis.

The night we return to our canyon
home, still burning stumps
star the blackened bluffs
like headlights where there are no roads.
Semaphores of golden light flicker
in stunning beauty, as if, from the heights,
some presence keeps watch.

II

What You Think Love Is

The Evolutionary Purpose of Heartbreak

Two weeks after Bert vanished
midway through the semester,
he appears in the hallway, jumpy,
eyes like red highways scribbled on a map
through treacherous country. He can't
come to class, he says, unable to sit still
or focus. A tortured glow unfurls
around him like battered wings.
Later in my office he explains.
It's about a woman, of course—
the poem he turns in late says
Her absence left a hollow
In the mattress, a ghostly impression.

Now she is back, in the flesh, to fulfill
their joint lease, but with another
man sharing her bed in the apartment.
He begs a chance to make work up,
which I grant and am tempted to offer a room
in my house as well, wishing to confer
some small comfort, since in the face
of heartbreak there's nothing
useful to say. Something has exploded
inside him, he says. Some yawning darkness
whose entry had been shut off, perhaps
since childhood, has blown wide open.
He wears the manic glint of a spelunker
about to descend. Scared. Resolute.

What You Think Love Is

The plane banks east out of Sacramento
as fields quilt into pattern—blocks
of green and wheat and smoking black
where a farmer just burned stubble.
The beginning of one homestead,
end of another.

Over Sierra forests boundaries vanish,
except for the cobalt Lake
Tahoe and, to its left, the green
oblong Lake Donner. Just north
lies a grove where snowbound
emigrants, tracking a new life,
famously devolved into cannibals.

Only ninety miles from Eden
their roadside memorial
confirms the path of the heart
treacherous: no map, no hawk's view
of the journey's end. Would it have been
better to stay put, die warm
in a comfortable bed? How can it be

trusted, the fox trail that leads
through pines and blackberry brambles
and the loud silence of a blizzard?
When the bloodhound heart hears *come*,
by scent alone
you enter the woods.

And whether love, in the end,

is beautiful or brutal all depends
on what you think love is—
how strictly you draw the borders.

Prodigal

Here, on the doorstep, is the heart wearing rags. Frayed cap
pulled over the ears. Prodigal that has frittered its fortune
loving best what it loses. Wanton, it has been rapt

by the arms of a saguaro's silhouette on a tangerine
desert sky, the vision fading to glare long before noon.
One night as a teen at Island Park, the lake glassine

as an August moon rose over pines, I lay on sand
with a boy poised to kiss me when a loon
trilled a warning I did not yet understand.

That fall, his name on the evening news—killed
when his brother, crouched behind him, fired too soon
at a buck stepping into view. So grief was instilled,

its mourning dove piping countless times
over the years. When 300 whale calves are found strewn
along the coast of Patagonia, their deaths chime

the cracked bell in my chest. A quail's upturned twig-
legs in the road. Apple blossoms hail-battered and hewn
into sodden drifts. A humpback's song silent. How big

must the heart grow to hold the lost, the suffering?
Is its work to break a little each day? Is that how it blooms,
opens to take in more, fasten on everything?

Never

Once in his father's mint-green Caddy
we parked in the foothills, above the Babel
of expensive houses climbing toward heaven
along the creaky Wasatch Fault. The Salt Lake
Valley spangled like a night sky shaken down.
In the distance the lit temple we aspired
to save ourselves for shone beside the Mountain
Fuel sign, a flaming MF over the holy city.
I didn't get the joke. Either one. Atop Walker
Bank a neon cross forecast weather—blue
for fair skies, orange in a storm.

Inside, on that roomy front seat, the season
was variable. My dress, my bra
had been designed for a tempest, but his fingers
were nimble, his tongue wind-driven fire.
My breath was silk ripping. The windows
fogged, then ran with rain. Our lips bloomed
into red spring peonies. My licked nipples
froze to snowflake points. Below,
a summer ocean throbbed.
Long curls of dazzling waves
stayed just on the edge without ever cresting.

Angel of the First

I am the good angel of the first fuck.
The good angel weeps tears no one can see.
—Philip Dacey

Poor broken, crippled thing—one wing
hanging limp, fractured like a ruined
statue. Hair bleached and bristly
as a desert skull. Eyes hollowed out
shadows that flash stars.
He can't be blamed for clumsiness
as new lovers knock against each other
in the hungry dark, all elbows and knees
and blind crevices. The awkward
places he must inhabit render
even the heavenly arthritic: crouched
in cars, steering wheel carving
an inkless tattoo. A salvaged sofa
in a musty apartment, springs poking up
like buckled bones. Icy ground
of a cemetery, the dead gaping blankly on.
As the young fumble for something
like ecstasy, the good angel bends over
them, not fluttering so much as bumbling,
his one true wing a drawn curtain, cupped hand
sheltering match flame in wind.
Yes, he weeps, silently, invisibly.
He weeps for the dreams that die here.
For the ones that begin.

The Fool

My sister, the psychologist, says that donning
a costume to live as another
self, for even a few hours, can change
and heal one, revive something
of the shadow, the lost underworld.
So for Steve's Halloween Party I planned
to be The Fool, that silly innocent
from the Tarot about to step merrily off a cliff
in her curly-toed shoes and Robin Hood hat, mindless
of the harrowing plunge into matter.
But the persona that arises is Bunny,
whose stand-up ears are secured by a headband
that holds in place her bright auburn wig.
She wears black fishnets and silver heels
found at Goodwill for three bucks.
The 42 double D bra I paid two for she fills
with six pairs of socks. In her fuchsia leotard
topped with pink satin bolero, bottomed
with pom-pom tail, she is a hard-living woman
who chain smokes Kools and swigs Jack Daniels
out of shiny flasks Archie and Jughead offer
from their hip pockets. I pay for her sins tomorrow.
I'm working out my slut complex, I tell friends
who at first sight don't know me. It's no secret
Bunny's bodice is puffed with athletic socks,
but men still leer and I laugh in Bunny's tinny voice
and she shimmies her ass dirty dancing
because her gangster partner, Clod, has tucked
in the waistband of his double-breasted-suit trousers
a long-nosed plastic Ruger. I'm safe in her disguise.
We win the prize, Bunny and I—a gold pig trophy—

in two categories: the costume most out of character and the one nearest to naked.

Shameless

after a photo in Life *magazine, 1944.*

If she is still among the living
and not in some bone heap like those found
a few months later at Auschwitz, this woman's hair
would by now have grown white
and airy as dandelion fluff. In the photo
entitled *Leaving Chartres, 8/44,* it has been shaved

by the mob who mean to shave
her spirit, too, strip as much life
as they can and still leave enough to photograph
her public shaming. She was found
hiding with a month-old child, cracked white
walls for company. The dark-haired

infant clutched to her breast (hair
the mother's shade before it was shaved)
is half German. On the woman's white
forehead an inverted V brands her for life,
like the death camp tattoos found
on survivors. Do those spitting in the photo

know her secret? Did the photographer
see she had come within a hair
of being led off one night like others found
out to be part Jewish? The clean-shaved
soldier with a swastika on his sleeve kept her alive
with his attention. It must have seemed white

fate, him noticing her in a plain white
blouse waiting tables. Even in this photo
her beauty smolders like a coal. Vibrant, alive,
she was sixteen, and when he touched her hair
a spark flared. Too many close shaves
to refuse his advances, so she found

a way to love her enemy. She found
herself abandoned as France was liberated. Clicking white
cobbles, one black shoe after the other, shaved
head gleaming, she walks into the photo's
perpetuity without apology. While her hair
grew back she wore a scarf, then vanished into a new life.

Still, this moment of hell, an amazing find by the photographer—
the woman's white skull more striking than hair,
her dignity unshorn—goes on redeeming her miss-taken life.

Sorting the Seeds

Psyche sits in charred chaos, past weeping.
Only his last words still burn. All was lost
in the blaze when her lamp oil spilled, scalding
his perfect bronze skin. Did Eros construe

it a mercy, inflicting no greater
consequence than his absence? What could
punish further? Strewn on the granary
floor, vetch, millet, lentils, wheat, barley, beans,

a billion bits of an exploded dream.
No clue to sorting them. But the ants pity
her, little Virgos compelled by passion
for order, each ruptured hymen restored.

After completing two more hopeless chores,
she'll earn her pass for hell's requisite tour.

Eve Considers Her Wedding Vows

When I gave them
there was no other choice—
companion, lover, destiny.

Why then turn the world
into a lush orchard of fruit
we forbid ourselves?

Marriage a pleasure
boat? No. It is a skiff
for lost and driven souls

seeking a place called Eden.
Isn't that where we were sailing
when we promised *forever*?

Why haven't we arrived?
Windless journeys, exotic shores
always at mirage distance,

rocky coasts too easily
discovered. Every port
offers some fresh beauty

to startle the heart anew.
Ampleness of apricot in bloom.
Sweetness of ripened peach.

Each temptation springs another leak.

Star Clusters, Not Constellations

The woman blamed herself for her inability to believe.

Butterflies fluttering close by are said to be souls
of the dead trying to make contact.

In a dream, her dead brother didn't recognize her.

The snowfall that year was so great it was measured
on phone poles. Tunnels shoveled to the sidewalk, garage.

She believed people who believe the Bible
to be the literal word of God lack imagination.

She stopped making her bed but still had to lie in it.

Two cars parked so close together the doors couldn't open.
They said goodbye through rolled down windows.

A fantasy kept playing in her mind:
he was saving up the good news for last.

Depression, she had told him, is a tantrum of the ego.

Maybe things don't have to add up, fragments
being the steady state of the human condition.

After weeks of storm it was a shock to catch the moon's
razor of brightness in the persimmon sky.

Another Way of Saying Goodbye

Your fingers fidget a pulled sweater thread
into a little whole as you sit together on the porch
letting the chill of dusk take you. Later

you'll wonder: did your friend take offense
at some crooked glance or crack you'd meant
to be funny? Or did the poison of a small

neglect make *you* start seeing slant? Something
casual and unremarkable as blue jeans.

It isn't like a wave catches you unexpectedly
propelling you headfirst into sand. More like
a faucet drip nibbling at your threshold of patience

or pity. A grave dug a shovelful at a time,
over time. A shadow falls out of a closet, so subtle
you don't feel the grip on your ankle pulling you down.

In the way that color recedes as night comes on,
her face seeps into the background.

You are sitting right next to her when she disappears.

Oldies

How did he chisel into my dream last night
long after I'd sworn I was through trying
to reach him? Was it the ultimatum
I laid down with my head on the pillow,
saying God, grant some clarity here?
There he was, brighter than yellow tulips,
as if last week's chill hadn't killed
everything in the garden.

This morning two ripe tomatoes hunch
beneath a tangle of wilted vines,
and an acorn squash emerges, finally visible
with its canopy collapsed in a slimy heap.
Every autumn the same surrender
to lessening light, the struggle to let go
a season subsumed
in earth's recurring dream.

Like Indian summer he comes back, a tune
from the past on a radio playing in another room.
The notes melt, like frost glazing the grass,
my resolve to forget. I cut late chrysanthemums,
amber and plum, to brighten the kitchen table.
As long as he's here he may as well stay
for supper. In the dream I was laying another
plate. Making him up a bed.

The Fall

i.

Stepping from the elevator on the hospital's third floor
she hears the hollering, but doesn't identify the storm
of construction-worker curses skirling off the walls

as her husband's particular invective. Fat cells stored
in the marrow, when the femur shattered, swarmed
into the bloodstream where, not small

enough to pass, they now rupture capillaries that feed
the neo-cortex. Small explosions afflict the lungs as well,
which is why he's rigged with oxygen. Pin dots

measle his torso. The doctor must be able to read
his symptoms clearly, fearing brain cell
damage, his outbursts perhaps indicative of a clot.

So painkillers have been withheld pending more
observation. A nurse in ICU intercepts her in the hall
to say it's common in young adults, explaining his delirium.

She watches him twist in agony, this man she adores,
although his motion is sharply curtailed with both legs all
strung up in traction, weights like some Luciferian

torture device dangling from the bloody plaster boot
on each ankle. In some nightmare or memory
he yells at his mother, angry and swearing, as if, rather

than yesterday's thirty-and-something-foot
fall onto concrete, she is to blame. He swats the pesky

fly of his penis tearing loose the catheter

before wetting himself. Then escapes this hell
by passing out for a short, merciful spell.

ii.

When he wakes his wrists are tied to bars
on the bedside to prevent his tearing the IV
again from his bruised inner arm.

He seems calm and lucid and asks in his regular
gentle way if his hands might be set free.
But that refused, he goes off like a fire alarm.

He begs her to untie him, and demands
to know why she's so heartless, so mean.
Toward evening, alert, burning with pain,

he tells her he can't bear this no-man's-land
any longer—he needs a shot of morphine
or will have to go away. He doesn't explain.

It is she who then does the begging, and when
at last an injection cools the fire
in his bag-of-marbles heels, he sleeps not having said

he's planning to stay. A resident hands her a pen,
asking for her number in case a trache is required
while she's gone—one more contingency to dread.

A student nurse she knew in high school, sorry and polite,
lets slip it's not expected he'll last the night.

iii.

At home she sleeps hard, without dreams—
she'd miss the ring should someone call—
and awakens slowly, forgetting he's not there

until, stretching, she feels the cold seam
down the center of their bed, unnatural
spaciousness instead of his warm, bare

body against her. Reality invades.
She dresses slowly, choosing a dark, wool
skirt and sweater, something proper

for a 21-year-old widow in case that grenade
explodes today. But his death is annulled
for now. Although no one is yet sure

he'll fully recover, there's been a small
improvement. Still ghost-pale, he smiles
and opens his eyes when she touches his hand.

Each day she sits until long after nightfall,
keeping her ineffectual vigil while
he mostly sleeps. Like tip-toeing quicksand,

this waiting to learn if his bones will mend
enough to allow him to walk
again. He was a basketball star

in high school, and played left end
during football, an all-around jock.
That super-hero pose has slipped far

over the horizon. His aliveness has always drawn
her. She wonders what else of who he was is gone.

iv.

After ten days his bed is wheeled to the ward
where he'll spend months on his back in traction.
At least he's beside a window where,

awake before dawn, he stares, already bored,
as daylight spurs a city into action.
She brings the morning paper and combs his hair,

two of a thousand things she tries to lift
his spirits. She ignores her boss's frown
when she lengthens her lunch to visit at noon.

Nothing much matters but the gift
that he's alive. The Christmas countdown
comes and passes, the new to full moon

cycles. Some evenings she reads aloud
while he drifts on Demerol: James
Michener's *Hawaii* plays out in living color.

Through the four-person ward, a crowd
of freak cases moves. One aims
to daily dump his urinal using for

target his food tray. An old vet with a stump
for one leg lets his hospital gown ride
up so his shriveled privates hang out.

A biker, who got drunk and dumped,
shattering his shoulder, lets loose a tide
of curses at nurses when he flouts

the rules and they take his booze. He chain-smokes.
Across the hall, a paralyzed kid in a circular bed
was crushed by a steamroller. Bad as things seem

it's not hard to find someone with a worse stroke
of luck. Her husband is healing slowly, not dead.
He reads, marks time, and dreams

of going home. When x-rays prescribe more lying
in traction, an aide pulls the curtains to conceal his crying.

v.

Fast forward three weeks: he comes home in a wheelchair.
Forward a year: more surgery and months relearning to walk.
People from church come to visit and declare his healing

a miracle. They praise Jesus, citing the Bible where,
with a touch, the afflicted one is all fixed up. Baby talk,
she thinks. For suffering, along with the faith-repealing

witness it compels, alters perception. The known
is redefined to fit a new, harsher vision. It takes
decades for the love of God to grow enough to encompass

unimaginable pain. A lifetime to peacefully own
the body's frailty. What had been seen as the self breaks
the way river reflections shatter when a bass

leaps. Standing in slow current thirty summers later,
her back to the failing sun, she sees on the slick
surface light ray out from her shadow, as if flesh

eclipsed a radiance she'd never imagined, a greater
self. The man with a limp, upstream, who flicks
his fly-rod, looks so little like the fresh

young stud who-she-used-to-be used to love.
When a fish jumps, the ring of its re-entry swirls
the salmon cloud wisps streaking a silver

riffle. Swallows dip and rise around and above
her. After sunset the water turns to pearl.
The world, over time, has somehow grown lovelier,

and life intensely precious—not paradise,
but, in the end, mostly worth its outrageous price.

III

Living in Flesh

Fireweed

This body offers to carry us for nothing—as the ocean
carries logs . . .
                                   —Robert Bly

Broken tree trunk, cut off from the primeval forest—
sweetness of cedar, birdsong sifting the shadow mosaic—
washing down a hillside toward rushing water. A voice
hungry for the named world into which we are born.

+

Sunflower. Tumbleweed. Wild wheat—parched plumage
on the canyon rim edging a desert town. A child, I sit
on an outcrop tossing stones toward Parley's Creek
glinting through the scrub oak. Red ants stinging my legs
make this body mine. Weed fire. Fireweed.

+

A log's washed onto the beach I walk at dawn near Goleta.
An old pelican stands hunched, well back from the surf break,
crookneck hidden, head pillowed on the breast. Hovering
over the bulwark of a woody beak, his eyes surprise me.
No fear lights in them when I pause beside him.
Further down the strand, a hump in the sand
some gray feathers pierce through.

+

Fireweed grows well in burned or logged areas. It favors
roadsides, avalanche areas, waste places.

+

When we arrive, it is all going on without us. Ocean engine
already rumbling. Fallen awns of wild wheat bend
and unbend their chevron bristles to the day's humidity, stroking
like a frog to hollow a bed for its seeds. Tumbleweeds scatter
thistles as they roll in wind. Sunflowers follow the sun's arc.
Heliotropism. *Helianthus.* Its pattern of florets a Fermat's spiral.
A Fibonacci sequence. As if by naming some claim could be mad

+

On Goleta Beach three shorebirds poke wet sand to feed.
The largest with a curved beak twice as long as the others'.
Adaptation of species. Plover. Sandpiper. Curlew.

+

After atomic bombs exploded over Nevada,
tumbleweed was the first to grow back over ground zero:
an invader once called tartar thistle, introduced
by Russian immigrants.

+

When we arrive the world is already named.
In the left frontal cortex, Broca's Area is primed
to produce language, Wernike's
hard-wired to comprehend it. A brain fixed
to accommodate concepts: the idea of freewill.
The notion of a self. Flower heads tracking sun.

+

Turquoise winks from the damp sand: a broken shell,
iridescent and stained in pearly waves. I pick it up,
put it in my pocket. Carry it home. Even though its color
was perfected for survival, or by chance, I call it beauty.
And this body, which carries me for nothing, quickens.

My Big Left Toe

It was the ark that redeemed my animal
urges when, like the flood-washed
earth, my eight-year-old-body
was plunged under the baptismal flow.
Unreborn, unrepentant,
my stubborn big toe stuck up
bearing forward the seeds
of my transgressions.
When I emerged from water
supposed to start me purely over—
wet, white pajamas creased to my behind—
each barefoot step cast a seedpod of sin.
As I grew exotic plants sprouted,
lush hybrids of my childish wrongs
with blooms like fleshy orchids,
Venus fly trip, creamy berries of mistletoe.
Iniquity veined each scintillating leaf.
My fruitful planter's toe
made me capable of anything.

Subtle Devils

Hours unknotting my down-the-back mane,
wild with its weekly washing, those Saturdays

when I was seven: unnoosed strands matted
and clumped as though my ponytail

had scratched on a post. *Do you want me*
to bring out the clippers and shave you bald?

Mother would snarl when I shook away
or cried. She muttered and yanked

and ripped at my tangles
as though she was exorcising a demon.

I was taught young to watch out
for the sly snares of evil—told,

should a spirit appear in my dark basement
room, how to sort Satan from saint.

Not by his scarlet vestments, by horns
or batwings: devils are subtle and take human form.

But a spook is obliged to obey
certain etiquette: you offer to shake his hand.

A holy ghost declines, unwilling
to tarnish his light with flesh.

Mother worked hard scrubbing our stains.
Dial soap on my tongue for calling my brother a shit.

Clothes hanger to beat the sass from my sister
like she was a hung-up bathroom rug.

General Store, Garrison Utah

After a photograph by Carla Resnick

The loneliest road in America ends here: General Store
at the edge of a long desert. Inside, worn hardwood floor.

The child I was still waits here with six coins tied
in a hankie that smells like the rose petal sachet inside

Grandmother's dresser. Real copper pennies, a hint
of serpentine bearding Lincoln, tarnishing the print

that spells *One Cent*. She stands before a glass case
filled with rainbow-colored candies, for grace

has allowed that some will be hers. Atomic fireballs,
banana chews, licorice whips, root beer barrels,

lemon drops, Smarties, candy Lucky Strikes.
Her favorite, white crisps with skinny brown stripes,

named peanut butter something I can't recall.
But my tongue remembers the crunch and the animal

joy of working loose sweet crystals stuck in a molar.
She takes her time, each choice voiding another.

This place holds a story that can't be left behind or put
to rest because it doesn't yield, even pressed, its nut

of meaning—the what-happened-next, the why.
Sidewalk hot on small bare feet, a cloudless summer sky.

Every particular seems significant and yet
nothing does. Traveling back one may forget

there are landmarks and ghosts to be passed through,
sticky webs of a younger self who speeds toward the blue

horizon as if to escape gravity. Destination unknown,
she barrels past on the highway, windows rolled down,

singing with the radio that fades in and out over miles.
In love with the wind and with the honey ache of exile.

Sterling's Silver

Papa said the grandfather I never knew,
who died five months before I was born
on his birthday, wasn't much
of a family man. He stayed away a lot,
disappointed when my uncles
all took to drinking. Maybe he was just tired
by the time my father came along, youngest
of eight, who never touched a drop.

Papa told me how his father
would make the pre-dawn milk wagon
run from Woods Cross to Salt Lake.
He'd sleep on the way back, trusting the horse
to find home. One morning it stopped
on the tracks of the old Bamberger Line.
The horse was killed and Grandfather
was laid up for months recovering.

Papa said his father had mining
in the blood. Maybe it was his name,
Sterling, that drew him to search
for treasure in the earth, always craving
something more precious. He spent
a fruitless season prospecting for gold here
in California, by Whiskey Springs
near a place I've camped.

Papa told me he remembered seeing, at sixteen,
a year before his mom died of cancer,
the check in his father's hand:
four-hundred and thirty-nine thousand dollars,

his share of the dairy finally sold
to a brother. This was in the mid-thirties,
Depression years. Every single cent lost
gambling for silver in a Utah town named Eureka.

Snowfield

Almost lost in the white, Mother was not
much more than a crease in the sheet, snapped
limb drifted over by snow. Her marbled
inner arm, tied to a splint, bared a smudge
of veins to a needle's fang. Plastic tubes
skeined to inverted jars hung on thin chrome
wings, an angel, or raptor, hovering.

A cart stacked with silver domes delivered
her Thanksgiving feast—a little beef broth,
spoon fed by Father. Someone had to help
hold up her head. Balanced on the edge of her
high, wheeled bed, I could feel her too-big heart
beat hard enough for us both. *Careful*, she
winced, when I kissed her snowy cheek goodbye.

China Closet

The china closet my grandmother gave
me when I married wouldn't fit
in the Ryder we packed to the roof—
though a fake Christmas tree was saved,
wedged in very last—so I left it
with a friend I left behind, proof

of my screwed-up sense
of values. I had painted the deep
oak turquoise, trashed the glass
doors, and, the final offense,
covered the shelves with cheap
flowered Contac paper: my crass

idea, at nineteen, of decor.
Our green Fostoria goblets
sparkled in the mirror
that backed the top shelf. Four
years later it migrated from dinette
to baby's room, a modest terror,

it turned out, for my daughter.
A photo records how she climbed
in, not quite a year, and,
like a surfacing otter,
bobbed straight up, crying each time
her head struck wood. By hand

my friend stripped the oak
to its natural honey, sanded and oiled
the shelves, made the glass side panels shine.

Visiting, I admired the piece. The joke
was I didn't recognize it—unspoiled
now and beautiful—as mine.

It's still yours, she said,
if you ever want it back.
But careful labor had made
it hers. Not seeing what lay ahead,
I was glad for her to keep it. I lost track
of my legacy over the decades.

*Firewood becomes ash. It does not
turn into firewood again,* goes
an old koan. The sage said more:
*But still we should not
hold the view that would suppose
ash is after and firewood is before.*

I want it back. In its wholeness,
before I unscrewed the doors of glass.
Before I opened the can of satin-gloss.
Before I became grandmotherless.
Before the friendship turned to ash.
Before *after* became just a word for loss.

The Mountain Lake Notebook

Reading the notebook I kept at thirty-three, I grieve
a little for who I used to be.

Water was her compass that summer, and, though she doesn't bar
the fact in these pages, she would skinny-dip whenever urge

and opportunity hooked her, her longing an underground spring.

I want the voice to stir deep within me,
like a stone sinking so far down I can barely hear it
thunk the bottom of the well.

Needing to feel one with Earth, she hiked the Sierras,
Sandoz's *Crazy Horse* tucked in her backpack for trail guide.

When it grew too dark to read, she wrote by firelight:

Ear pressed to the ground, the Lakota boy could hear buffalo moving
two ridges away. We are separate from earth the way that boy was
separate from the buffalo hooves singing in his ear.

At water's edge, she smeared yellow mud over her body in the hea
of the day. Dug with bare nails wild onion to stir into her soup,
    feeding sticks onto a fire.

Granite cliffs edged a mountain lake where possibility could be
measured by the reach of sky. She held her breath in its presence

Each time I enter wilderness something is reborn. Waking
at first light, warm in my bag, I watch snow-cap turn vermilion
in the silver lake, swallows swooping.

I miss her combination of wisdom and naiveté, her faith
in there being a real answer to uncover. Her hope she could

fuse language with mystery so completely stones would speak.

How did she know things I don't? She left
these words for me to find after she was gone:

History is encoded in the body: an ocean beats in the blood.
The point is to live everything, lives left behind, whatever's separate
or over. Don't refuse any aspect of your past—

only live to discover the way it was true.

Will

When my daughter's birth was late
three weeks I became a desperate woman.
I jumped off the porch, drove a truck
fast over dusty, rutted roads, and
swallowed castor oil in orange juice
to get things moving. Which it did.
But not the stubborn one
clenched in my belly, shy snail growing
more reticent the more her shell
was prodded. I began to doubt:
false labor—false pregnancy?
Finally I resigned to being amorphous.
A rainbow ringed the moon
that midnight I paced the sidewalk
pausing for contractions. At dawn
she emerged, boldly, filled
with the force of her own will.
And I, who had questioned her way,
lay back limp, in awe
at her cream-slicked skin, at the greedy
way she sucked her long fingers,
impatient for more, ready to devour
whatever milk her new life offered.

Green Pasture, Still Water

You lie in bed, a baby's low gurgles saying
what fingers patting your breast means.

He smiles up between sucks, and you tell him
you will always hold onto this moment,

Even when you are a grown man, you say,
palm cupping his little bottom.

But as he's nuzzled close you know
the furry head and heat of this small body

are only now. Know memory can't grasp
the body's truth except as a longing

toward it. Just as you've found
contentment, placid in the lush meadow

of his being, you are already giving him up
to become himself, as you, in turn, will be

given back to yourself. Stranded once more
on that rocky shore. Does it ease the ache

to know some of his fetal cells
will live in your bloodstream for decades?

That, as a man, his presence will be sun
pouring through an open door?

Twenty-odd years later, at the Seascape
Cafe—a table with a view—

you spot a seal pup stranded
on the stony beach, hear its mother

barking in the bay, watch as she dives, swims
back and forth across the cove searching

and you feel again the stab of separation.
The pup lifts head and flippers in reply

but can't crawl as far as the water.
The sun is setting. Hours before tide turn.

His destiny is uncertain.
There is nothing you can do.

Proud

Out on the track at 6 a.m. seeking
absolution for yesterday's deadly sins—
the Gold Rush Ale, the tequila, the
Symphony Bar, king-sized, with almonds, and
Uncle Ed's Vegan Trail Mix Cookies that got me
through a long, rough day. I dismiss lofty
glances from the three goddesses, younger
sisters to Isis, with their glistening
ebony arms, whittled waists, glorious
breasts immune to gravity.
Talk to me about it in thirty years,
I think, huffing around counting laps—
five jogged, three walked to regain
breath, if not dignity. Their godlike coach,
also Egyptian gorgeous, a true work
of physics, sits on their feet for curls,
presses their magnificent shoulders close
to the ground when they stretch, legs split into
nearly collapsed V's. *And now ladies,*
let's see some wind sprints I hear him call
as I turtle across the line for round six,
and they arise on his countdown to sprint
like the wind, its ease and grace. And as I
make the final turn telling myself one more,
you can do it, avoiding the eyes
of the gawking coach, he pipes up
you should be proud of yourself, you should be
proud of yourself, you out here doing it,
that's the thing. I breeze the final circuit,
the booze diffusing into the sweaty
air, chocolate melting, my short,
white, lumpy body almost forgiven.

There Was a Question about the Sky

When I say relax into joy,
I don't mean dance
in a field starred with daisies
and lupine, hair flying wild.
I don't mean the abandon
of a child spinning cartwheels
on fresh-mown grass.

I mean joy that simmers
on a back burner, flame ringing
the black disk barely visible,
aroma of clove and apple
warming the house like a promise.
The copper-bottomed pot can't help
shining like a shy bride.

It's a discipline, sensing beneath
homely disguises the ordinary
assumes. Ditch water bubbling
from a shadowed culvert chitters
like quail in the blackberry thicket.
In Morse-code the heart converses
with life, vital but mostly unheard.

When I listen, shivering pines
say yes, yes, yes, yes
to the simmering breeze
between full-boil gusts
that rearrange everything.
How astonishingly blue fierce
wind leaves the deepened sky.

Kindness

A curious celebration, the birthday,
commemorating a term as trapped light.

It works free with a hacksaw called age.
The mirror discloses blade marks:

striations embellish the triceps, for instance.
They inspire aspiration—press

weights, practice yoga, revive
muscle tone, the image always urging

be more, be other. Push-ups
may be uplifting for the boobs

as well, although during this spring's
scan for cancer the technician

assured me all breast tissue
finally evolves to fat. Still,

they are sweet, dangling shyly,
shrunken little mothers stroked

with silver, containers for kindness
so full it would take a moon spilling

into a lake to hold it. Two moons.

Living in Flesh

It comes to you at an odd moment, sitting
on the bed tying your shoes, the dog taut in the hallway
awaiting her walk. That face, the serious but sweet
furrowed-brow of the yellow lab, is wholly trained
upon yours, anticipating the cues, the ritual moves:
knotting back the hair, slathering lip balm, unwrapping
a stick of gum, and the final, joyful confirmation, your hand
gathering the leash. And you suddenly see
how the body which you call *me*, by your own name,
is a way to focus consciousness, yours, which, if it exists
somehow, somewhere, sometime
beyond or before the body, you have all but forgotten.
And it seems to have lost track of you as well,
although some smoky tether must still secure you.

Walking, you understand the body
is a means of slowing attention: to finger the timothy—
shoulder-high, leaning into the road, ferny tips ripening—
while the mind flits hither and yon, into next week,
to the camp at Flaming Gorge, then around the globe
where your daughter sails the Mediterranean.

A gray fox bleeding from mouth and nose, red strings
and globules, innards that erupted upon impact,
snaps you back. Like the creature that zipped
across the canyon road last night, caught
for a moment in your brights, so swift you had to guess
what the silver streak was. You'd wished for a closer
look, more detail, and now here, the long, stippled fur
and stiffened legs, blond-streaked plume of tail,

smaller than you had imagined,
so slowed you can scarcely bear to look.

And the consciousness its fox-body tendered?
A smoke puff dissipated—into what?

You think then of the giant redwoods,
having hiked among them just days ago,
who have held their gazes more
than two thousand years, surely aware
though not in a flighty, human way.

One tree's ringed memory measured seven yards across,
its shagged bark two feet thick, feathery top too tall to be seen
where you stood at the base. It had grown
from a dark pinhead: profound concentration
like a black hole
expanding into a universe.
Its one-pointed, whole-hearted attention
focused right here, right now.

Wine with Lunch at the New Year

The conversation slips easily from what it costs
to get married to what it does to die. And then a host

of morbid speculations. My earth-sign friend plans
an ecological burial, a way to give back, to become

compost feeding some new life—lifted
up by oak or gladiolus. I'd want a view, near a cliff

edge like the one suicides drive off near my canyon home.
But the thought of lying underground almost hurts. *Burn*

me, I say, at which my friend shivers. *You're born of air,*
she observes, *and so feel at home in the wind, not scared*

of blowing off unrooted. But of us, as us, does anything
go on? After a car plunged over the edge last spring—

a lovelorn teenage boy it turned out—my daughter woke
at midnight to the dog growling and a sense of presence. To block

possibility, we rimmed the house with a line of salt.
It's a new year, resolution time when we're tempted to assault

ourselves with fresh beginnings. And only one year more
on the Mayan calendar. We're all at death's door

one way or another. Still, I can't quite imagine my own
absence, really believe in my demise. Going home

the spirituals call it. Despite the years I've struggled to accept
this body as safe dwelling, it *will* burn down, its ashes swept

off in wind. Like the one that drives cold rain this morning
hard against the windows. The dispossessed wanting in.

Omega

Driving Nevada, Early February

Ahead, a ghost shape broods over Battle Mountain,
rolling amoeba-like toward the interstate. The sun,

low in the west behind, licks the cloud mass, turning
its edge into a ragged rainbow, a passage through

a needle's eye, closing: my daughter's prayer blesses
my father as he moves toward *the grey rain curtain*.

We enter a blizzard—whiteness whirrs around us for a mile
or two then opens onto stars and the unknown

he is becoming. The night sky sweet with the bouquet of it,
a field blooming. Wind's low voice mothering a new silence.

Blue

Cobalt, sky, baby, sapphire, royal, cerulean,
color of my father's ice-cracked eyes startling open

in pain or panic or outrage every ten seconds
as his emptied body does what it must after

the brain's been oxygen starved. All that's left
of thought is this lightning storm, ceaseless,

like the primal days of Earth before the heavens
steadied. Even with his terrible quaking

I am grateful to see these beautiful eyes again.
Even though I know they still can't see me.

Ground

My sister and I hold one hand, an i.v. needle protruding,
Mother clasps his other, as though steadying him

over rocky terrain. The whole landscape
of my father's life sucks back to his breath

thinning, so gradually we scarcely notice
it cease. He has come to the cliff edge

where he must fall or fly, no retreat.
Does he fly? To his Mormon heaven?

Into a new life? Or does he go underground,
subversive, present only by absence?

Star

Now that he is nowhere I imagine him everywhere,
like that first, that primal thing, in a black nothing

listening. All parts of him now are wild,
spread like numberless small eyes

upon vast silence. Point to him and the sky opens.
Each of us who knew him composes a separate fiction

with a common ending: he's moved beyond the body's
ruined shelter. Will the last night of earth be this—

winter stars through wind-scrubbed glass disclosing a light
come home to the heavens? That star I followed here.

Orbit

for papa

Rounding the dark star it orbits, your death's
anniversary concludes a broken season.

My bones feel a little drunk on the growing light,
amnesiac winter relaxing towards thaw.

From frost's chrysalis no winged thing is emergent,

but the resilient ordinary
promises to flower.

Gone a year, tonight you dream nearer

like a panther or the soul
gazing from the edge of a far jungle.

I'm beginning to believe you could still come to my rescue.

Your fidelity glows like a hearth.
In the warmth of this safety

I keep you. I let you go.

The Journey Ends with the Child

Midway down the dried path
of middle age, it grows rocky and steep,
cliffside plunging, the aftermath
of sea chewing headland for eons. A sweep

of guano-iced crags in the bay marks
where land's end used to be. All
that's known unravels. You still embark
now and then upon the philosophical

sport of staying up late to haggle, over wine
of course, profound abstractions like
Karma and Consciousness, until you decline
into quandary, at last agreeing to strike

a friendly truce and trundle off to bed.
Sleepless on the pillow your brain
still revs, as if it could spread
wings and fly from its boozy haze to explain

why you had the fortune to be born
well and grow sleek in a land of plenty
rather than in Bangladesh, a country shorn
daily by the tide thieving twenty

more miles of cropland, where every third
infant starves. And then you know for sure
this is, as the Buddha said, imponderable—absurd
to suppose you could solve the puzzle or secure

your boat to a pier that pounding waves
won't finally splinter. You rise and walk outside
in the dark where a soft hand of mist laves
your face. Damp deck wood guides

your bare feet to the edge. The night
is swaddled in fog, half-hearted breakers
sound in the cove. Your plight
is you can see nearly nothing. If there's a maker

that knows all, it must be a force remote,
disinterested, heartless, and wholly wild.
Still, tonight you feel cradled, swayed in a frail lifeboat,
a well-loved, radiant, nescient child.

Notes

How the Story Ends. Beyond War was an organization active during the 1980's, Reagan years, whose focus was educating people about the nuclear threat and promoting the understanding that war has become obsolete as a means for problem solving. *Out on a Limb* is Shirley MacLaine's autobiographical exploration of reincarnation.

Hawk Flight is in memory of Jackie Hall and for Jo Ellen Hall.

Early Narcissus is for Barbara Kniffin. Thanks, Bob, for letting the story be shared.

Two Lines Borrowed: the opening line is from a poem by Lalla, a saint and mystic who lived in 14th Century India. The last line is from Rumi, the 12th century Sufi poet.

Never is for Gary Thompson, Utah edition.

The Fall is for Jerry

China Closet is for Dorothy Solomon. The koan referred to is from *The Genjokoan,* written in 1233 by Eihei Dogen.

Will is for Danielle.

Green Pasture, Still Water is for Jacob, Victoria, and Briana.

There Was a Question about the Sky: the title is a koan. This poem is for John Travis, who offered it.

Wine with Lunch is for Carole Oles.

The Journey Ends with the Child: the title is taken from John Tarrant's book, *The Light Inside the Dark*. This poem is for Beth Spencer.

About the Author

Joanne Harris Allred was born and grew up in Salt Lake City, Utah, but has spent most her adult life in California, where she taught for many years at CSU Chico. She lives in Butte Creek Canyon outside Chico with her husband, two dogs, a variable number of chickens, and a lush companionship of wildlife. Her previous poetry collections are *Whetstone* and *Particulate*.

CPSIA information can be obtained at www.ICGtesting.com
Printed in the USA
LVOW11s0336090914

403157LV00001B/29/P